MANAGING WITH
CARROTS

MANAGING WITH
CARROTS

Using recognition to
attract and retain the best people

ADRIAN GOSTICK & CHESTER ELTON

O. C. Tanner Recognition Company

Salt Lake City

05 04 03 02 01   5 4 3 2

Copyright © 2001 by O. C. Tanner Company

Published by
Gibbs Smith, Publisher
P.O. Box 667
Layton, Utah 84041

Orders: 800-748-5439
www.gibbs-smith.com

Design by Rich Sheinaus/Gotham Design, NYC

Library of Congress Cataloging-in-Publication Data

Gostick, Adrian Robert.
    Managing with carrots : using recognition to attract and retain the best people /
Adrian Gostick & Chester Elton.—1st ed.
        p. cm.
"Including case studies of powerful employee recognition experiences in some of
North America's finest companies."
    ISBN 1-58685-077-6
1. Incentive awards—United States. 2. Employee retention—United States. I. Elton,
Chester. II. Title.
HF5549.5.I5 G693 2001
658.3'225—dc21
                        00-012605

To Jennifer and Tony
To Heidi, Cassi, Carter, Brinden & Garrett

Whom we recognize
as the most important people in our lives.

CONTENTS

ACKNOWLEDGMENTS

Thank you to:

Our O. C. Tanner colleagues:

- Kent Murdock
- Cyndie Rodman
- Tim Treu
- Clark Campbell
- Kevin Salmon
- John Pingree
- Greg Boswell

Our editors:

- Christie Giles
- Glen Nelson

Our contributor:

- Randall Shirley

Our researchers:

- Lori Janes-Young
- Greg Boswell

Our publishers:

- Gibbs & Catherine Smith
- Christopher Robbins
- Madge Baird
- Melinda Rhodes

Our designer:

- Rich Sheinaus/Gotham Design, NYC

The Blonder Family for their help in developing our theme.

The companies and people quoted within.

INTRODUCTION

"Oh carrots are divine"

— B. Bunny, from the cartoon *Robot Rabbit*

There's a crisis in business today: The rhetoric we've been using for years—about people being "our most important asset" —has actually come true. Without much warning, we woke up one day and realized that, in this competitive marketplace, having the right talent is the key to success. Go figure.

This new situation not only leaves us vulnerable to the whims of our formerly faithful workforce but is costing us a bundle.

Just look at recruiting expenses. Companies are offering enormous incentives to land the right people. Many are giving their employees bonuses of $25,000 or more if they recruit a friend or colleague to work at their company. Others are spending tens of thousands of dollars on signing bonuses, relocation, training and development, and early pay increases, only to lose a good percentage of their new people within a few months. (See *figure 0.0.*)

Source: American Management Association Survey, January 11–18, 2000, 1,548 respondents.

Spending big bucks on retention doesn't hold much water either. Many companies are giving employees what they say they want—large salaries, bonuses and stock options—but still suffer 20- or 30-percent turnover a year.

Now, money as a management tool does seem to make sense at first glance. We all love the stuff. And our employees certainly seem to tell us that they want more of it. In theory, money should retain and inspire.

But it doesn't. Money doesn't buy love, it doesn't buy happiness and it doesn't buy commitment.

Of course, to successfully manage and retain employees we must offer competitive pay and benefits. That's a given. But too many organizations are trying to manage by what we call "bread alone." They offer above-average pay and benefits, the "bread" if you will, and expect that to make up for the significant shortcomings of their work environments. But today's worker will not stay at a job—and certainly will not stay committed to a job (even a good-paying, prestigious one)—if she's not satisfied.

Here's the proof: In the largest study ever conducted on workplace satisfaction,[1] good pay and benefits were not even ranked in the top twelve items that make up the most satisfied, profitable and productive work environments.

What topped the list? Carrots. Our employees are craving things such as:

- Knowing what is expected of them.
- Having the tools to do a good job.
- Having the opportunity to do what they do best.
- Receiving recognition or praise for good work.

While corporate America is desperately slicing the bread thicker and thicker in an effort to satisfy their employees' seemingly insatiable demands, employees are literally starving for carrots. And the most powerful corporate carrots are recognition and awards.

When done right, recognition becomes an effective retention tool, enhances communication and trust, and improves employee productivity. The power of effective recognition can spread through your company like wildfire, creating a culture of recognition—a place where people are willing to put down roots because they know their contributions will be acknowledged, appreciated and rewarded.

In this book we look at the role of strategic recognition in the corporate world and explain how today's worker can be motivated most effectively with carrots. In the first part of this analysis, "Carrot Seeds," we speak to the corporate need for recognition. In the second section, "Carrot Planting, Carrot Cultivation," we explain how to set up an effective recognition program. In the third part, "Carrot Harvest," we describe the benefits of implementing a carrot culture, as we clarify the human benefits of recognition. In part four, "Starting Your Own Carrot Crop," we help you begin developing a carrot culture. Along the way, we present our discoveries of what has worked for the best managers in some of the best companies.

In today's competitive crunch, nothing beats carrots. Stick with bread alone, and you might just end up toast!

PART ONE
CARROT SEEDS

"Can you dig it?"
— John Shaft, from the film *Shaft*

Why recognition?

*Recognition is the most powerful strategy
your company can employ to achieve better business
results and retain your best people.*

North American businesses are becoming increasingly concerned about their ability to retain key personnel. Today, turnover is at a ten-year high,[2] and the average worker stays at his job less than three and a half years.[3] For a company trying to stay ahead in a competitive world, this decline in commitment is at a crisis level. It could be the difference between corporate survival and death.

From the high-tech world to traditional manufacturing to the finest service companies, there are only a couple of certainties in business today—the pace of change is staggering, and you need people who can develop solutions that will help you stay ahead of the crowd.

And that means the tide of power is beginning to shift in your organization—away from those with grand titles toward those with knowledge, ideas and commitment. But your most effective employees—those on the front lines and in management positions—are being courted and coddled by the competition. And many are being led away.

"Unemployment in the U.S. is at a record low and has created both a scarcity of available professionals and a feeding frenzy that has firms scrambling to recruit and retain their competitors' key employees and executives," says Brent Jespersen, a partner in the executive search firm The Diestel Group. "Human capital has become the key element to success in the new economy, and companies are desperate to find and keep good talent. The organizations that keep the best people are going to win—it's that simple."

FIGURE 1.0

Help Wanted
Executives believe there is a scarcity of skilled labor

65% of managers characterize the current availability of skilled labor in their industries as "scarce."

Only **1%** of managers consider skilled labor "abundant."

64% of managers are "more concerned" or "far more concerned" about employee retention than they were the previous year.

Only **6%** are "less concerned."

Source: American Management Association 1999 Survey: Staffing & Structure, 1,192 respondent firms.

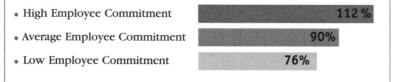

FIGURE 1.1

Commitment Creates Profits

Companies with highly committed workers deliver
much higher returns to shareholders

A survey of 7,500 people finds workers who are highly committed to their employers and have confidence in top management
deliver dramatically higher returns to shareholders. However, only
about half of workers polled say they are committed to their employers and even fewer have confidence in senior management.

3-YEAR TOTAL RETURN TO SHAREHOLDERS

- High Employee Commitment — 112%
- Average Employee Commitment — 90%
- Low Employee Commitment — 76%

Source: WorkUSA® 2000 Survey, Watson Wyatt Worldwide, 7,500 workers.

To react, you've most likely read a few articles on successful
retention tactics. You may have even tried a few of the most com-
monly quoted tactics—work/family balance, strategic compensation programs, enhanced teamwork, casual dress, and so on. But
almost without fail, every business expert's laundry list of ideas
for keeping your good employees—and keeping them focused—
fails to include the most important item: recognition.

Few of these experts know that there is a demonstrated correlation between workplace satisfaction and employee recognition, or that recognition is the most effective way to further your

corporate goals, or that by creating memorable recognition experiences you can bond an employee to your organization.

We have surveyed tens of thousands of employees in an attempt to measure and understand employee opinions on recognition and what makes an effective recognition program. And we've discovered a few simple truths.

First, the good news: Many of the world's best organizations have carefully built cultures of employee recognition and awards, and their efforts have been rewarded with well-documented increases in employee satisfaction, productivity and profitability. According to a recent study of 3 million employees in 551 large companies,[4] only 14 percent of organizations surveyed view their people strategy as a source of competitive advantage. But those companies that had an effective way to recognize employees realized a median total return to shareholders of 109 percent between 1996 and 1998 versus 52 percent for employers that didn't. That's a two-to-one margin.

These organizations successfully align every element of the recognition experience with corporate objectives and values; they train their managers to make effective, memorable presentations; and they include appropriate corporate symbolism on formal recognition awards and throughout supporting materials—helping to create a bond between employees and the company.

And, now, the bad news: Many companies have no idea how underappreciated their workers feel, and many have no idea what their workforce wants. These employers wonder why most of the front line mopes around the plant, criticizing every new initiative. They wonder why so many leave for new jobs that pay just pennies more an hour. They wonder whatever happened to the good old days, where loyal employees put in an honest day's work for an honest day's pay.

While many of these companies compete for the best employees with pay, promotions and other enticements, too often employees are looking for something simpler: They want recognition. If you ignore that human longing for corporate carrots, you fall prey to a hard statistic: 79 percent of employees who resign their positions cite "perceptions of not being appreciated" as a key reason for leaving, according to a recent survey conducted by the Society for Human Resource Management.[5]

Frankly, it's quite depressing.

So, instead, we present a love story.

On a winter day in 1998, pharmaceutical company Warner-Lambert (now joined with Pfizer) brought its 40,000 employees together to announce quarterly earnings.[6] Leaders in 140 locations walked up to podiums simultaneously. Each leader told his or her respective crowd that the company's amazing six-year journey from middling performance to industry leadership had produced spectacular quarterly earnings. In recognition of the Herculean effort, all Warner-Lambert employees across the globe would be presented with an award to thank them for their contributions to the company's remarkable success.

An HR manager in a Dublin, Ireland, plant, whispered to a colleague, "I hope it's not a T-shirt."

The Dublin general manager continued his presentation: "While we have achieved record numbers, what is not apparent to the outside world is what stands behind those numbers: More than 40,000 colleagues around the world with a single purpose and a common vision."

Especially, said the general manager, he was thankful to the Dublin employees who had achieved such outstanding results. Then, one by one, each employee was called forward to accept a fine watch with a custom engraving that read "We're making the world feel better"—the company's theme line.

A Dublin biochemical operator accepted his award and said, "The [engraved message] is a mark of what I've contributed to the company. If you buy a bracelet for your loved one, you inscribe something on the back as a mark of the way you feel. The inscription on the back of the watch comes across as the way the company feels about my contribution."

Okay, maybe it's not much of a love story; but it is a success story. According to Warner-Lambert executives, the award and presentation were enormously effective and generated *thousands* of letters of appreciation to the CEO. Said one company official, "It brought Warner-Lambert to the world stage in terms of employee recognition."

Only six years before, Warner-Lambert faced daunting business challenges, lackluster results, lagging share price and threats from stronger competitors. At the time, the new CEO asked the world-wide workforce to make sacrifices, refocus priorities and reclaim the company. He asked employees to embrace change, to be more responsive to customers, to improve quality and to lead the market.

But just as importantly, the company leadership also pledged to change. The CEO and his key leaders became more supportive of employees' basic human need to be appreciated and recognized.

The latest earnings announcement made it clear: The company had become one of the strongest pharmaceutical and consumer-products companies in the nation. Only months later, Warner-Lambert would join with Pfizer to create the fastest-growing, most valuable pharmaceutical company in the world.

Unfortunately, Warner-Lambert's tale is just that to the typical employee, a fairy tale. They haven't yet found a company where they can live happily ever after.

Let's take a look at Susan, a good performer in a typical corporation. Behind some closed door, she's identified as a keeper. She earns a healthy salary and year-end bonus. Her boss will reach retirement age in a few years and it seems obvious to everyone—except Susan—that a flashy future looms, with even more bucks, perks and travel. But still, within six months, she ends up bolting to the nearest competitor.

Why did Susan leave? Ask her, and chances are she'll admit that her former company "wasn't a terrible place to work. The pay was good, and in time might get better. It's just . . .?" After a moment she rubs her chin and starts to talk about her garden.

There's a very good possibility Susan can't put her finger on the problem, or is too embarrassed to admit she didn't want to spend her professional life without any recognition of her contributions.

Carrots: A Weekly Necessity

In 1999, the Gallup Organization released its findings of a twenty-year study into workplace effectiveness. The study revealed that there are twelve key dimensions of great workplaces, dimensions that consistently correlate with work groups that have higher employee retention, customer satisfaction, productivity and profits.

Items one through three were knowing what is expected of you, having the tools to do a good job, and having the opportunity to do what you do best. Item four on their list was receiving recognition or praise within the last seven days for doing good work.

In fact, Buckingham and Coffman, authors of "First, Break All the Rules," cited praise and recognition as essential building blocks of a great workplace. They are right, of course. On the most fundamental level, we all need to be recognized as distinct human beings and to feel we add something unique and positive to our surroundings. But those criteria typically receive the lowest scores on employee attitude surveys. Said the Gallup authors:

Turnover Takes Its Toll

Turnover—as in a sugary pastry or a new leaf—is a good thing. In business, turnover is a huge drain on the bottom line.

Experts estimate that it costs up to three times the previous worker's salary to replace an employee. Many mid- to large-sized companies will spend $40,000 or more during an employee's first year on training, mentoring and supplying that employee with all of the tools and knowledge needed to do the job properly.[7] The cost of replacing a highly skilled professional or a leader in your organization can often be $100,000 or more—and that doesn't include the loss of intellectual capital that results from each departure.[8]

Historically, praise and recognition in the workplace have been handled from the perspective of, 'If you don't hear anything, assume you're doing a good job.' In contrast to this 'old industrial workplace' mindset, the new knowledge-based worker relies and depends upon praise and recognition as the means of defining what is valued by the organization. Today, praise and recognition are communication vehicles for what is deemed as important.

The worst possible thing we can do to someone at work today is ignore him. Just as our bodies need food, employee psyches

However, even given those sobering numbers, turnover rates in most companies increase every year, according to a survey conducted by the New York–based Conference Board.[9] The study showed that while most companies use direct financial compensation as a retention tool, they should be focusing on strategies such as offering:

- New opportunities
- Recognition
- Skills training
- Formal career planning
- Enhanced benefits and services

According to the researchers, most of the surveyed HR executives believe that rewards and recognition are vitally important. And many of these senior people were embarrassed and apologetic that their companies were not offering more.

need a steady diet of daily recognition or their energy, commitment and trust fade.

By the way, are you planning to eat anything today? After all, you did eat just yesterday.

Get the point?

Why Carrots?

Okay, enough of this touchy-feely stuff. Employee feelings aren't reason enough to change the way you do business, right? Well, here's some food for thought.

In the corporate world, recognition is used for one reason: to drive more business. While it may sound mercenary to some, it's a reality. Corporations cannot survive if they do not make money. Shareholders demand it. Workers demand it. Suppliers demand it. And since costs keep rising every year, and workers and shareholders want to be paid more every year, the company must make more money every year. Thus, your employee-recognition culture must recognize people for doing their jobs a little better today than they did them yesterday.

And while every company has its unique motives for affecting this behavior, carrots are typically dangled to:

- Reach company or departmental goals or objectives;
- Recognize outstanding achievements;

- Boost morale;

- Increase productivity and profit margins;

- Increase profits and drive more business; and/or

- Keep good employees.

You'll notice that we've put "reaching company goals" first on the list. If you have recognition programs that do not lead to fulfillment of the company's goals, they should be reevaluated—and fast.

PART TWO
CARROT PLANTING,
CARROT CULTIVATION

What are the key elements of
successful recognition?

The best recognition creates
experiences that bond employees
to an organization, align employees with
corporate objectives
and explain corporate symbolism.

Praise and recognition come in two forms: informal and formal.

Informal recognition is immediate and typically inexpensive. It involves a thank-you card, E-mail or public acknowledgement.

Informal recognition has a huge potential to positively impact your organization, and it costs just peanuts. Most employees would value a regular E-mail or visit from their boss, saying how much they are appreciated or even how they can improve their performance. And who wouldn't love to be asked, "How can we better recognize you?"

Here are a few simple ideas for supervisors or managers that can pay big dividends on a day-to-day basis in your organization:

- If you have reserved parking and an employee doesn't, let her use your spot for a day or two in recognition of an outstanding achievement.

- Buy a coworker or employee a free cup of coffee on the way to work. Fifty cents can go a long way.

- Send a voice mail to your boss praising a coworker. Copy the employee.

- Give an employee tickets to the symphony or a ball game for a job well done. Make sure you rotate the gift throughout the entire department.

- When making routine visits to the CEO or division higher-ups, take along an employee in recognition of his/her efforts.

- Make sure that informal recognition occurs within earshot of other employees.

- Ask for opinions on projects you are working on. This shows employees that their ideas are important and valid, and you'll get some great ideas you wouldn't have thought of on your own.

- Start every meeting by recognizing someone in the department. Ask the employee to recognize someone else at the next meeting.

- Have a casual day to recognize a significant team accomplishment.

- Send out department-wide E-mails telling coworkers about an employee's or team's important contribution.

That's informal recognition. It sounds simple, doesn't it? But we've found that the corporate culture where this really occurs—on a daily or weekly basis—is rare. When people do find this kind of culture, they tend to stay.

Our extensive research addresses **formal recognition,** an area that has not received anywhere near the attention but has just as great an impact on employee retention. In fact, formal recognition is absolutely critical when building a culture of recognition in a company.

Formal recognition includes performance-based awards; service, sales and safety awards; new-employee recognition; and so on. But these formal carrots are often poorly thought out, and too many organizations have allowed these incentives to become entitlements. Even companies with well-established recognition programs often botch opportunities to create powerful, bonding "recognition experiences" during the formal-recognition process.

What are recognition experiences?

Imagine you've just won the Olympic Decathlon—congratulations, by the way—and you approach the podium to receive your gold medal. Your head is swimming with memories of the endless hours of training, the immense sacrifices of yourself and your loved ones. You recall some early failures and remember that you nearly gave up many times, but something inside urged you to continue well past what you thought you could achieve.

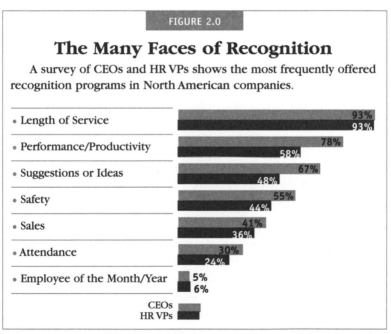

FIGURE 2.0

The Many Faces of Recognition

A survey of CEOs and HR VPs shows the most frequently offered recognition programs in North American companies.

- Length of Service — 93% / 93%
- Performance/Productivity — 78% / 58%
- Suggestions or Ideas — 67% / 48%
- Safety — 55% / 44%
- Sales — 41% / 36%
- Attendance — 30% / 24%
- Employee of the Month/Year — 5% / 6%

CEOs
HR VPs

Source: "Employee Recognition: A Vital Ingredient in American Business," Executive Insights, *Wirthlin Worldwide, Spring 1997 Special Issue.*

When to Offer Carrots

New-employee orientation is the best time, most experts agree, to begin the formal-recognition process. A small award during the first few weeks on the job helps bond a new hire to an organization and helps retain the employee during the stressful training period.

Service awards or career achievement awards—generally presented to employees every five years—are used by more than 90 percent of companies in North America. Service awards are the foundation of effective formal recognition.

When done right—within the right recognition strategy and with the right presentations—length-of-service programs are a perfect opportunity to recognize *every* employee in the organization, open communication channels, and build relationships between management and employees. These awards also appeal to a basic human need employees have to be included and respected, and they also provide validation to all employees that their efforts do matter and that the company is aware of the "thousand little things" they've done over the years that no one has ever acknowledged.

Service awards can be enduring symbols of achievement when they feature your corporate identity.

Retirement recognition is another standard at most companies. But gone are the days of presenting a gold watch at retirement. Today, most companies offer a selection of items that allow employees to choose their awards—from traditional gold watches and rings to grandfather clocks and electronics. A beautiful, symbolic retirement award can be the capstone of a career—something that will be treasured for years to come. And what is said in a retirement presentation has tremendous potential for positive impact on the heart and soul of the recipient—who will continue to be an ambassador for your company—and perhaps most importantly on coworkers who are present.

A **performance-recognition** program should be much more than a "thank you" for a job well done. When implemented strategically, performance awards advance the corporation by recognizing behaviors that support the company's core business goals. The recognition may come in the form of a simple note of appreciation or a public ceremony and the presentation of a quality award. Employees or teams may be nominated and recognized by peers, other departments or a manager for actions that help achieve significant results, such as:

- **General Performance:** Creating innovations, developing patents, reaching operational milestones, humanitarian achievements, etc.

- **Sales:** Achieving overall or area sales targets, winning new accounts, retaining your best customers, upgrading existing customers, selling a specific product, etc.

- **Safety:** Working a certain length of time without accident or incident, the accomplishment of specific safety training, hours driven without accident, etc.

- **Attendance:** Working a significant number of hours without absence.

These programs are important to an integrated recognition strategy that helps foster the commitment of your employees. Which programs you choose to implement will depend on the culture and primary goals of your organization.

You step up onto the podium. Your nation's flag rises and the national anthem, which you have heard a million times but never as gloriously as this time, resounds through the stadium. The dignitary slowly comes near, leans close to you and whispers, "Your medal is being sent to you in the mail. Here's a certificate, though." You look down to see your first name is misspelled.

Sorry to say, that's how many organizations treat their best employees.

Corporate recognition awards can truly be enduring symbols of achievement—earned in appreciation of dedicated years of service or for outstanding contributions to an organization's success. But the best organizations have learned that they must make a recognition event something memorable—with almost as much ceremony and emotion as an Olympic-medal event.

PRESENTING CARROTS

You've probably seen or been a recipient in a typical award presentation.

It's finally arrived: your fifth anniversary at your company. At last, you are vested in the retirement plan. You're going to get a good parking spot. You arrive at work all excited in anticipation of the big event.

But the day passes without any fanfare. Just as you are ready to head home, your boss sticks her head in your office, tosses in a package and says, "Here's your service award. By the way, did you get that assignment done?"

What could have been a day to remember has turned into a disappointing experience. For the company, a chance to create a meaningful, bonding experience has passed.

According to an O. C. Tanner survey of more than 33,000 award recipients in the United States and Canada,[10] an effective presentation makes a significant impression. In fact, the

---

FIGURE 2.1

Presentation is Everything
An effective award presentation makes a significant impression

97% of employees felt their "contribution was acknowledged" after an "excellent" award presentation

39% of employees felt their "contribution was acknowledged" after a "poor" award presentation or no presentation

93% of employees felt an "excellent" award presentation "built commitment"

41% of employees felt stronger commitment to their organization after a "poor" award presentation

presentation of an award affects employees' perception of the entire recognition program, even their perception of the company as a whole (see *figure 2.1*).

When surveyed employees called their award presentation "Excellent," 97 percent of them said their "Contribution Was Acknowledged." Which, of course, is exactly what you want to happen. You want people to feel valued and appreciated. You want them to feel bonded to your organization. But consider what happens when the surveyed employees called their presentation "Poor" or when they had no presentation. Given those scenarios, only 39 percent of recipients felt their contribution to the company was acknowledged.

Time to hang the "Help Wanted" sign out again.

Now, let's say your recognition program's goal is to build employee commitment. Some 93 percent of those surveyed said "Excellent" presentations "Built Commitment." Only 41 percent of those who had "Poor" or "No" presentations said they had stronger commitment to their organization after receiving their award. Presentation quality had a strikingly similar impact on ratings for "Communicates Company Culture/Values" and "Increases Productivity."

When asked about "Overall Satisfaction" with their job after an "excellent" award presentation, 80 percent of employees were positive.

Obviously, strong presentations can make a remarkable difference in your recognition program. But what makes an effective presentation? An effective presentation does not mean holding an elaborate banquet or other costly event. In fact, the best presentations simply involve a manager who takes the time to prepare in advance.

Here are a few presentation tips:

First, choose the right person to make the presentation. That doesn't mean picking the highest officer in the company. Too often, the CEO fumbles when he tries to pronounce the recipient's name or doesn't know anything about the person's specific accomplishments. To ensure sincerity and meaning, the presenter of the award should be the highest-ranking manager who personally knows the employee and his or her accomplishments. The person must also be able to evoke emotion—whether with laughter or tears—through anecdotes or examples. For recognition to work, it must evoke feeling in the recipient, in coworkers and in the presenter.

Second, ensure your managers are trained in making great presentations. They must know exactly what is being recognized and talk about specific contributions that have affected the company. They must learn that an award presentation is a time for carrots, not sticks. They must make only positive, upbeat comments, focusing on the very best things that happen in your workplace and how the recipient fits into these good things that are happening. Managers should also be trained not to promise continuing employment, not to tell off-color jokes, and not to make discriminatory remarks. While you may think such training might be officious to some in your organization, it is, in fact, quite necessary. Handing out recognition in an effective manner does not come naturally to most managers—even those on the most-lofty rungs of your corporate ladder.

Who Should Present a Carrot?

Many employees distrust management. They believe coworkers first, immediate supervisors next, and upper management always last.

One study indicated that 43 percent of all employees are not just suspicious, they firmly believe that senior management lies and is trying to cheat them.[11] That's not just a few crackpots, that's four out of every ten people in your company! In contrast, a similar study showed that 96 percent believe their immediate supervisor is always or normally telling the truth.[12]

Workers need recognition, and our experience tells us that they will receive it best from their immediate supervisors and coworkers. And our research, refined from the experiences of thousands of companies throughout North America, indicates that the best managers celebrate almost everything—from meeting short-term goals to winning customers, from extraordinary work to safety successes—and they do it in an integrated manner.

SIDELIGHT

Third, if your program includes corporate symbolism, ensure that your managers understand and can explain the symbolism on the award and can tie the symbolism into the goals and values of the company. When your company logo is crafted into a gold emblem with precious stones, the manager should explain the significance and value of the emblem—and how this illustrates that the company values each of its employees.

Fourth, invite colleagues to attend the presentation, and ask two or three coworkers to comment on the recipient. Inviting

The Gallup Organization, in its 1999 survey, found a strong correlation between employee attitudes and critical business outcomes. What became clear to the researchers is that while we tend to celebrate great companies, in reality, there are only great managers. It's on the front line that the work of building a strong workplace really gets done.

That means the impetus for recognition rests squarely on the shoulders of front-line managers. Companies and senior management also have an important role, but it is in giving their managers the awards and training to effectively recognize and reward their best teams and best people. Senior management must help create an atmosphere that makes employees enjoy being at work, they must provide departments the support they need to do it right, and they must exemplify the practice of recognition with their direct reports.

But remember, most employees typically will not change their behavior based on anything but direct input and/or recognition from their immediate supervisor.

others to participate helps coworkers better appreciate the performance being honored, helps them more clearly understand company goals, and helps them emulate successful behavior.

Fifth, allow the recipient to make a few comments. Not everyone will want this opportunity, but every recipient should be asked. This gives the employee a chance to thank others who have helped along the way, to thank those who participated in the recognition experience, and to provide direction to others in attendance who wish to achieve similar results.

Sixth, close by offering a sincere thank-you.

Follow these six simple steps, and employees will eat it up. That's the goal at Tricon, parent company of KFC, Pizza Hut and Taco Bell. At Tricon, management feels so strongly about recognition that it's near the top of their corporate mission statement. "Recognition: We find reasons to celebrate the achievements of others and have fun doing it," comes right up there with "Customer Focus" and "Belief in People."

When Tricon employees are recognized, they do it right. The company even has a Recognition Band that marches in to celebrate a randomly selected person's achievements in a very big way. Tricon managers carefully prepare for each recognition event. They've been taught to work hard to tie specific recipient accomplishments to the company's success, and they have a good time.

"It's all in the presentation," says Debbie Riggs, who heads up KFC's recognition efforts. "You have to have fun with it. If an employee receives an award in the mail or somebody flings it on the desk, the award will have little meaning. The presentation gives us a chance to say, "Thanks. Now, here's how you've done a great job...."

Another company that stresses effective presentations is Johnson & Johnson. J&J's suture supply company, Ethicon, recently presented every associate (their term for employees) with an award during the company's fiftieth-anniversary celebration. To make the celebration effective, the company trained managers to make a presentation that would link the award to individual, team and company accomplishments.

"If you look at the Fortune 500—even the Fortune 100—of the last fifty years, it's amazing how many of those companies don't exist anymore," said Donald Bowers, Ethicon's director of public affairs. "Here at J&J, we've had a unique kind of success, which happens because we've got extraordinary people doing extraordinary things for us."

To celebrate the fiftieth anniversary, we helped write a brief script for each manager. Then associates gathered in small work

Donald Bowers, *Ethicon's director of public affairs, believes in handing out the praise.*

groups and talked about the history and accomplishments of their company. Finally, managers presented every associate with a watch, thanking them for their efforts.

The award has been extremely well received. "Associates think it's the classiest gift and the nicest presentation, and they're proud to wear it," Bowers said.

But what if you have too much on your plate to devote much time or effort to award presentations? Like your mother said, put carrots first. The fact is, an effective recognition program is critical to your corporate health.

"There has been a lot of discussion about 'We're too busy these days and the awards should be sent to people's homes,'" said Bowers. "As long as I'm involved in the program, I'll continue to challenge that approach. Recognition is too important to just send gifts to their homes. This needs to be celebrated between the manager and among the associate's team."

J&J's Bowers adds that a great presentation is a win-win situation for everybody. "The manager looks good, the company looks good, and it makes the employee and those witnessing the recognition feel good."

Which is exactly what happened recently at KFC when Chicago-area Assistant Restaurant Manager Alvin Moore received his five-year service award—a watch with a sym-

Regina Gilford and Adonis Chapel *serve chicken and recognition at their Chicago KFC location.*

bolic gold emblem featuring the KFC logo. Moore's manager had given him the anniversary day off, but Moore stopped by the restaurant anyway to see if he was needed. In the style that is standard at KFC, the entire work team gathered to celebrate his five-year achievement.

"The award means I'm doing something okay," he says. "The presentation means I'm liked by people, that we're able to get things done, and that they appreciate me as much as I appreciate them. The emblem was a nice touch, because when people see it they know I got something special from KFC."

Which brings us to symbolism.

___

SYMBOLIC CARROTS

Symbols have indelible power. Consider the symbols you see every day: your country's flag, a symbol of nationalism and unity;

the eagle, a symbol of freedom in America; the Mountie, a symbol of justice and truth in Canada; the cross, a symbol of sacrifice and eternal life to millions of Christians; the Olympic rings, a symbol of athletic excellence. These symbols evoke emotion.

In the business world, corporate logos and symbols can also have immense meaning. When people devote most of their waking hours to a company, they want to feel a connection. A corporate symbol can provide that link. It's one reason why companies spend millions of dollars to develop memorable, meaningful

logos. British Airways, for example, is reported to have spent 60 million pounds developing the marvelous yet simple logo it unveiled in the summer of 1997.[13]

When Lucent Technologies, Inc, was spun off from AT&T, it spent a considerable amount of money and effort to develop and unveil its red brush-stroke "ring of innovation" logo.[14] The corporate spin-off had created a great deal of anxiety for Lucent's employees, and the new logo helped these folks understand what was expected at their company. The ring was continuous—symbolic of the new company's commitment to continuous innovatio'

Another positive with the new logo: Many employees saw the hand-drawn design as very human and friendly—quite unlike most corporate marks.

Your recognition program's symbol might be your corporate logo or company name, or it might be something that represents your culture, such as a ring of excellence, a symphony or sports

team, an eagle, a flag or crest. Whatever it is, your company's symbol transforms an award from "just a gift" into a meaningful, useful, lasting representation of the employee's accomplishments.

A corporate symbol can be featured on an award in a variety of ways—through engraving, through stitching or embroidering, or through the use of an emblem made of precious metals. In fact, when employees receive awards that feature *their* corporate symbol crafted in gold and featuring diamonds or other fine gems, the awards become, in effect, corporate "gold medals."

A recent survey shows that when an award includes a quality emblem or symbol, it gains "trophy value" that cannot be matched in any other way—not with cash, not with gift certificates, not with trips, and not with merchandise alone. An O. C. Tanner survey of 17,000 recognition-award recipients showed that 74 pecent of employees who receive awards featuring their corporate symbol felt the symbol enhanced the meaning of their award.[15]

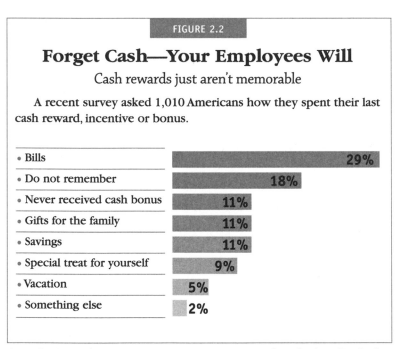

FIGURE 2.2

Forget Cash—Your Employees Will

Cash rewards just aren't memorable

A recent survey asked 1,010 Americans how they spent their last cash reward, incentive or bonus.

• Bills	29%
• Do not remember	18%
• Never received cash bonus	11%
• Gifts for the family	11%
• Savings	11%
• Special treat for yourself	9%
• Vacation	5%
• Something else	2%

Source: "Navigating the Incentive Construction Zone: Motivating with Merchandise & Travel Makes More Sense Than Ever," Potentials, quoting Wirthlin Worldwide study conducted for American Express Incentive Services, May 2000.

And when given a choice of including an emblem or not, 84 percent of employees choose to include their corporate symbol with their award.[16]

Take the example of a Fortune 50 financial management company, where employees are given a choice: an award with a logo or one without. At one point in O. C. Tanner's almost twenty-year relationship with this outstanding company, the organization was going through corporate upheaval and morale was quite low. Even during this trying time in corporate history, seven out of ten employees chose to have the company's logo on their awards.

Now, some will argue that the dollar sign is a very powerful symbol, and there is no question about that. We all need to pay our bills; we need to send our kids to college. But according to a 1999 survey, the number-one use of cash awards is to pay bills. And almost one in five employees will not even remember where they spent the money (see *figure 2.2*).

Money just isn't memorable. And it has very little power to motivate. Do you remember the amount of your last tax return? How about the amount of your last few cash bonuses? What did you buy with the money?

Then again, you probably can list every award you won in high school, even now that it's been ten, twenty or forty years since you walked those halls. Why? Because you received something tangible, and because you received it in a formal awards ceremony.

Without question, your employees will remember and use their symbolic awards for years to come. And unlike money, carrots in the form of symbolic recognition awards have the power to evoke real emotion. Every use will remind your employees of their achievements.

And you thought onions were the only vegetable that could bring you to tears.

Here's another example of a powerful symbol: In the late nineties we consulted on a recognition program for Novartis Pharmaceuticals. This organization was attempting to build a strong culture following a merger, and it focused on recognition as a powerful motivator. After much consultation, we called the recognition program "Ovations, A Journey of Recognition."

When the program was launched, Chairman Wayne Yetter and his management team talked continually about the journey employees were making together. When Novartis management spoke about the recognition program, they included a great deal of symbolic language about where the company was going and how it was going to get there.

As we looked for a symbol for this recognition program, we decided on a compass—a symbol of keeping employees "on course" during their journey. We then tied every element of the recognition program together with nautical themes. For example, teamwork awards have the symbol of a rowing team.

Since the program launch, the symbols have gradually become more important to Novartis employees as they have watched their peers be presented with awards and as company management has continually reinforced the importance of this program. Within the company, the compass has become a symbol of excellence.

Now and then we hear from a company that has tried unsuccessfully to incorporate symbolism into their recognition program. Without fail, we find that the company lacks an effective way to present the symbolic awards. The real power in symbolism comes in the actual presentation of the symbol and in communication surrounding the symbol. The best programs include outstanding communication—teaching employees how to achieve the symbolic awards and informing employees of the latest award recipients and why they received recognition. Communication and effective presentations send the vital message to the entire organization that we celebrate the excellence of individuals and teams that further the goals of the organization.

When carefully crafted and skillfully communicated, symbolism can help capture the hearts and minds of employees and dedicate them to the company mission and vision.

COMMUNICATING ABOUT CARROTS

Remember back to the summer of 1995, when moviegoers had their pick of an unusually large number of films? *Apollo 13, Pocahontas* and *Batman Forever* were among the big-budget films released with substantial fanfare in theaters throughout North America.

Did the best movie, the best acting and the best story win at the box office? Of course not. The trophy for the biggest box office success of the summer went to *Congo.* In July of that year, the *Wall Street Journal* published an article on the fate of *Congo* and a smaller film, *A Little Princess.*[17] Lisa Bannon of the *Journal* wrote, "Panned by most critics, 'Congo' nevertheless boasts a brilliant marketing and promotion campaign....A week before the film's opening, Americans were besieged by *Congo* subway posters, billboards, movie-theater popcorn bags, radio ads, an HBO cable special, TV ads, movie trailers, newspaper ads, toys, watches and a site on the Internet. Pepsi put 'Congo' jungle-theme designs on 17 million prizes. Taco Bell placed *Congo* decorations and billboards at 4,500 restaurants."

In short, *Congo* was everywhere. And despite reviews that were scathing, the film made more than $66 million in its first month.

By contrast, said the writer, critics called *A Little Princess* one of the best movies of the year. *Variety* magazine predicted the film would be "a classic the moment it hits the screen." Time Warner spent little on print and TV ads for the film but expected to benefit significantly from word of mouth and outstanding reviews.

The result? Word did not spread, the reviews did little to help, and *A Little Princess* was a box-office failure.

While there will always be a handful of exceptions—films starting slowly and building momentum through word of mouth—the vast majority of box-office successes come through clever marketing and distribution.

The translation for your recognition program? If you don't communicate extremely well, your recognition program is not going to be successful.

Unfortunately, too many employers never pull their carrots up into employees' view. As a result, really great recognition programs stay buried and ignored in piles of corporate mumbo-jumbo, while employers could be harvesting improved employee commitment, morale and performance.

You've heard that carrots improve eyesight. It's true that carrots have power to focus employee vision on company goals and strategies, but only if you link your recognition program directly to your goals and communicate effectively.

The trouble is, in many companies, recognition programs seem anything but strategic. To employees, they are unpredictable. Recognition seems to occur at random. And when it does happen, the fortunate souls are told, "You do great work," without any specific communication that helps them or their coworkers understand what they have done that is great and what they have done that helps the company. Are they punctual? Do they go above and beyond for customers? Do they meet production quotas on a consistent basis? Do they have the whitest teeth?

James Di Loreto at the Catalyst Group calls it the 2 A.M. test. "If you have communicated your mission and vision properly, any employee should be able to recite it to you without hesitation, even if wakened at 2 A.M. to do it," he says.

Says Howard Weizmann, managing consultant of the global HR consulting firm Watson Wyatt Worldwide, "You can have all the goals in the world, but if you don't tell people about them you're never going to achieve them."[18]

He went on to say, "There's a very simple premise: If you measure it, people will do it. If you measure it and [reward it], people will do it in spades. If what you measure matches up with corporate goals and strategies, the company will be successful. That in sum total is alignment. The most effective way to guide a company is through rewards strategies."

The best companies are beginning to understand that there are significant gains to be realized by linking rewards and recognition to specific goals and intended outcomes. And, just as importantly, these companies realize that their programs cannot be effective without strategic communication that helps employees understand what recognition and rewards they will receive when they do things that the company values.

At Prudential Insurance Company of America, for example, HR employees can be nominated for excellence.[18] While that could be a vague goal, the company communicates the specific characteristics it is seeking in its people through a steady stream of informational mailings, E-mail and company magazine articles about the recognition program. Then a video is created quarterly where customers praise the award recipients. The tape is shown to all 1,000 HR professionals across the country—helping reinforce the criteria of the program.

As Prudential and other top performers have discovered, in communicating about your recognition program, it is imperative to use as many vehicles as possible—written, electronic and face-to-face.

Written formats include:

• Program brochures (introducing award and nomination criteria)

- Award brochures (where recipients can select awards)

- Congratulations cards (another form of recognition for recipients)

- Thank-you letters (acknowledgment for nominators)

- Presentation training materials (helping managers learn the dos and don'ts of presenting)

- Home mailers (helping build excitement with family members)

- Monthly articles in the company newsletter (for program reminders, for updates and, most importantly, for success stories)

- Workplace posters, cafeteria-table tents, payroll stuffers, flyers and other creative reminders of program goals and successes

Electronic formats include:

- Internet- or intranet-based award brochures (featuring instant award selection for recipients)

- Intranet-program home page (for general program and award information)

- E-mail notification (featuring program reminders and recognition of award winners) with an automatic link to the intranet site

- Video (for program launch and ongoing success stories)

- Phone mail (for updates to the program from the CEO or other senior executives)

While it will be difficult for your program to succeed without written and/or electronic communication, face-to-face communication is the most important element of effective recognition. Typically, it includes:

- Executive speeches and walk-arounds (explaining the goals of the recognition program)

- Manager staff meetings (explaining team goals and providing updates on progress)

- Manager presentations (to recipients and coworkers)

- One-on-one manager/employee meetings (setting individuals' goals and reviewing accomplishments)

- Motivational speakers (to provide overall enthusiasm for the program)

If you are in senior management, you should be pleased to know that you play a critical role in this process. One of the most crucial elements of face-to-face communication is the executive speech and walk-around. However, you and your colleagues on the executive team must be in agreement on the goals of the recognition program and the overall importance of recognition before you hit the road. And you all must be dedicated to communicating the program goals clearly and consistently in public forums.

Part of that commitment and communication must also come in the form of recognition to *your* direct reports. Lower-level managers will not embrace this culture of recognition—and will not help you build value in the organization—if they don't receive praise, recognition and rewards from you, their boss.

Just as important as the executive speech and walk-around is the face-to-face presentation of formal awards and verbal thank-yous for excellent individual and team performance. As we noted earlier, if your managers understand how to make an effective presentation, they will help the individual or team understand how they achieved the award and inspire others to follow the example. But again, it is vital that you communicate with your managers about making good presentations. Help your managers by preparing them in advance of the recognition experience. Help them know how to deal with shy recipients, how to handle a presentation in a group with low morale, and how to use specific achievements to make the presentation more effective.

The best corporate communication links an employee to the bigger goals of the organization or division. Likewise, the best recognition programs should not only clearly communicate what behaviors or performance qualifies for recognition and what employees will receive for their efforts, it should also link individual accomplishment to company values and goals and help build valuable relationships between managers and their employees.

Stephen Covey spells it out beautifully.[19] Covey, one of the foremost authorities on workplace efficiency, says that building strong relationships with your employees is a key to increasing their overall commitment with your organization. He says the key to relationships is trust; the key to trust is credibility; the key to credibility is consistency. This consistency arises from tight alignment on vision, values and key objectives at the top; clear, achievable priorities in the middle; and open information sharing and dialogue at the work-group level.

Christine Luporter is director of communications at O'Connor Kenny Partners, Inc. She cites the example of how such a lack of alignment created havoc at one dysfunctional company.[20] The company Luporter was consulting with had employee turnover of 24 percent annually—at a cost of $7.5 million.

"After studying exit interviews, I found that a majority of employees were leaving because they didn't understand their personal future with the organization or how they fit into the overall organization," she said.

Luporter went on to say that people want to feel connected to and part of their company; they want to understand the organization's vision, values and goals, and they want to believe that leadership is effective before they will commit their full energy and effort. There is no better way for management to show their leadership than by developing, living and communicating an effective vision, she summarized.

And one of the best formats for sharing that vision is during a recognition experience, when recipients and coworkers are highly receptive to company messages.

FIGURE 2.3

CEOs: Why We Recognize

Desired objectives of employee recognition programs from a CEO's perspective

• Show support for employees	97%
• Enhance employees' attitudes toward company	96%
• Increase loyalty	92%
• Establish/Reinforce corporate mission	91%

Source: "Employee Recognition: A Vital Ingredient in American Business," Executive Insights, *Wirthlin Worldwide, Spring 1997 Special Issue.*

Here's a quick way to find out if your recognition communication is helping you reap a good harvest. Complete this sentence: "My recognition communication helps the organization meet its strategic objectives by _____."

The Productivity Formula

Great companies hire great talent, train them and motivate those people to high achievement by helping them understand company goals and how their contributions can help achieve those goals.

Today, *good* organizations understand that
productivity is created when:

ABILITY + TRAINING + MOTIVATION = EMPLOYEE PRODUCTIVITY

We call this the Employee Productivity Formula.

Of course, different workers are motivated in different ways. One of the most significant challenges in motivating your workforce is to build a recognition strategy that has the greatest impact on the greatest number of employees—not just your high achievers. To accomplish that goal, your programs must be communicated effectively. And in creating memorable, powerful recognition experiences, all communication within your program should reflect a consistent reiteration of corporate objectives.

In practical terms, that means your employees must understand your credo and mission statements. They must also understand how their jobs fit into the bigger picture. They need to know what is expected and what will be rewarded.

Thus, recognition is a process that must be continually communicated. At the most *outstanding* organizations, there is a new Employee Productivity Formula[2]:

ABILITY + TRAINING + MOTIVATION + COMMUNICATION =
SUSTAINED PRODUCTIVITY

Surf's Up—A Recognition Case Study

A few years ago, Atlanta-based BellSouth was one of the first companies in America to take employee recognition online.

Today, the company's employee-recognition site features service-
award communication and gifts with a theme that reflects the cli-
mate and values of BellSouth.

For a company that places a value on long-term employment and a
paperless environment, the site is a perfect blend, says Salem
Shunnarah, director of benefits delivery for BellSouth. "Our service
award program gives us one more way of reminding our employees
that BellSouth is a unique place to work, a place where employees
are valued and appreciated. We have loyal customers, and loyal and
committed employees are one reason why."

BellSouth employees who reach a service anniversary are notified
with a personalized E-mail. Then, with the click of a mouse, they
can order their awards from the convenience of their computer, at
work or home.

Employees who have not yet reached a service-anniversary milestone can still log on to the site and look at award choices, an
option that wasn't possible when paper brochures were mailed
only to employees who were eligible to order a gift.

Says Shunnarah, "Employees at BellSouth are beginning to embrace
this technology. We have been overwhelmed by the employee
enthusiasm for recognition on the Web."

If you can't complete that sentence in a compelling manner, your recognition program is most likely not as effective as you would like.

The best recognition communication:

- Explains the purpose of the program
- Clearly explains what actions are recognized
- Ties those individual accomplishments to the organization's vision and goals
- Details what awards are available
- Explains how to nominate a coworker or subordinate
- Fits the organizational culture
- Focuses commitment

The best companies communicate effectively. And the best companies realize that recognition communication is a vital tool in helping align people with business strategies.

CREATING A CARROT CULTURE

Moving to a carrot culture is not for wimps.

True change is a messy job, and usually the prevailing culture is firmly entrenched. To get rid of it, management at all levels has to dig in and get its hands dirty. Sadly, many managers would prefer to simply shout directions from above the fray, while their change initiatives slowly wither in the ground.

Employees know that.

They've been through enough of management's latest fads to know that few stick. They've cynically learned to play along, doing very little differently, until the next change comes down the pike.

Middle- and lower-level managers, too, are threatened by change. They have typically thrived under the "old way" of doing things and are worried that they won't be as successful in the new world. In the past they had many perks; they are concerned that the change will make them lose some entitlements. And, most importantly, they realize their jobs (not upper management's) are on the line if the change doesn't work.

But this latest change—to a culture of corporate recognition—must be different. It must be strategic in nature, it must involve employees, and it must be powerful and permanent.

John Kotter, professor of leadership at the Harvard Business School, has suggested eight steps to achieving organizational transformation.[21] We recommend integrating these steps in your evolution to a culture that recognizes and rewards employee contributions.

1. **Start at the Top.** Most change efforts fail because of a lack of commitment from the top and the lack of felt urgency, such as a competitive advantage to be gained. As a company leader, you can successfully make the transition to a culture of enhanced employee recognition and awards if you provide a sense to all employees that the company is moving together toward a better future.

   If you are in upper management, you must also build commitment to this cultural change with your peers. Too often we find that senior management may have signed off on the idea as a group, but a few members may harbor some cynical ideas about the benefit-versus-cost equation. Lip service by top management is the kiss of death for any change initiative. Given time, they may bring the entire program to its knees.

   If, for this reason, you do need more evidence of the human need for recognition, you may want to consider identifying your company's most-urgent needs with a baseline survey or focus-group discussions of employee/manager attitudes, issues and concerns. Or you may consider an examination of your industry environment, your company's turnover vs. competitors', employee exit interviews, or other criteria that will help you make a case to the holdouts in senior management. Only when they are convinced that this is war will the cynics be willing to climb down into the trenches with the rest of the troops.

2. **Choose the Right Team**. A small, strategic-change team must lead the process. And the team should be led by an individual who is passionate about employees and who has a powerful voice in the organization.

Involving people who manage blue-collar and professional workers will help ensure that recognition and awards are appropriate for every audience. It will also ensure that ideas from every area of the organization are heard—which helps build credibility and goes a long way toward cementing the program's long-term success. Without seeking genuine input, a change effort will be received with cynicism by the managers who must make this program a success.

3. **Have a Vision**. Next, working with senior management, the recognition committee must develop a "guiding vision" that will lead the recognition change effort. While your

recognition goals will be specific to your culture and your organization, your aim should be to create a culture where employees know their contributions are noticed, appreciated and recognized. Specific objectives in your vision should focus employee commitment on the things that matter most to your organization.

4. **Get the Word Out.** Effective communication will occur when all managers and supervisors feel involved in this change effort and fully support the corporate messages. And a well-articulated recognition vision must provide a way for employees to positively answer the question "What's in it for me?"

After the guiding vision for the recognition program is created, circulate it to every supervisor, manager and executive for input. When finalized, circulate the vision to all employees, with details on how the vision was developed: by a team of employees from around the company with the support of the CEO and senior management team. Follow this communication with implicit instructions on how the recognition program works, what will be rewarded and what awards can be achieved.

5. **Empower the People.** Change can't happen by proclamation or forced compliance. People must make the vision

their own. This means that division and department supervisors must then bring the overall corporate goals down to earth by writing specific objectives that their employees understand and are able to achieve. For example, if the corporation's overall goal is to improve customer service, the manufacturing department should be rewarded for outstanding actions that contribute to a customer's satisfaction—such as delivering products not only on time but with high quality.

Empowering your people also means that a recognition program should have formal and informal criteria, and peer-to-peer and manager-to-employee nominations. Everyone should have the opportunity to thank other employees for jobs well done.

6. **Create Victories Along the Way.** Changing corporate culture is a tedious, challenging process. Frustrations must be overcome with victories at every milestone. In the recognition change process, well-publicized awards banquets on a timely basis will keep enthusiasm high. Also, as we've noted earlier, publicizing success stories in written and electronic forms is a critical element to building excitement for the program.

7. **Never Stop Changing.** Even the best change efforts grow tired after a few years. Continually challenge assumptions and improve your recognition culture through measurement and training.

8. **Keep Proving Your Case.** As your organization overcomes the immediate urgency that forced a change, commitment to the new culture may fade. Your organization must continue to show how the evolution to greater employee recognition has contributed to improved performance, employee retention or other measures. Managers must continue to champion the vision and the new corporate culture of recognition and awards.

For a new carrot culture to take hold, the commitment must be complete. To be successful, strategic recognition planning should involve all levels of management, should clearly communicate how the recognition program works and what is recognized, and should involve training to help leaders make meaningful presentations.

Successful companies develop organized ways of offering carrots to their people. They build employee commitment with recognition programs that have one ultimate goal: to create powerful, lasting recognition experiences.

It won't be easy. But it will be rewarding.

"Leading the Drive" with Carrots, A Recognition Case Study

At Avis, recognition has a clear purpose: to enhance loyalty and commitment through recognizing the achievements and contributions of employees.

The company's award program, Lead the Drive to Preeminence, is an integrated system that recognizes achievement at four levels, with each level offering its own assortment of awards.

What follows is a summary of the Avis awards and recognition "Performance" system:

The **Starting with Thanks Award** is a spontaneous thank-you to a colleague who has performed well, gone out of his or her way, or been of special help. Recognition is immediate and sincere and serves as a reminder of how valuable great daily performance is to the company.

The **Horizon Award** is designed to recognize those who consistently make contributions that reflect the Avis Values and those who look for opportunities to improve the Avis Experience (customer service). Criteria for nomination include:

- Conceiving, developing and implementing new products and services designed to achieve brand and customer loyalty;

- Observable or measurable achievements that significantly and consistently go above and beyond the everyday scope of an individual's or a team's responsibilities;

- Making a significant process improvement that produces a long-term benefit to the work unit;

- Making a significant contribution to furthering one or more of the Avis values; and

- Contributing significant innovation or showing creativity in resolving a problem.

Horizon Awards can recognize a significant portion of the work-force in a given year. For example, Milton Currie, a bus driver, received the award after coming to the aid of an elderly man who was injured from a fall outside an airport terminal. Other recipients saved the company money, implemented new programs, built customer loyalty and provided outstanding customer service.

People like Currie add value at Avis. They are important to companies, but they rarely receive much praise.

Employees who receive the **Destination Excellence Award** make a significant, quantifiable impact on Avis's business. Employees reach this level of recognition when they:

- Develop an innovative idea for their own area that saves significant time and money;

- Develop an innovative idea that is successfully adapted to other parts of the company; and

- Play a significant role in attaining critical milestones that positively impact Avis.

The Destination Excellence Award is much coveted at Avis. Recent winners include a group of nine employees, who made an enormous contribution during the company's implementation of a new

"Leading the Drive" continues ☞

human-resources and payroll system, and the company's Hawaiian operations manager, Martin Mylott, who received the award for helping secure passage of beneficial state legislation.

Avis Milestone Achievement Award winners will be chosen from among the Destination Award winners, as selected by the company's executive committee. Winners will be determined based on the most significant impact on the business.

Horizon, Destination Excellence and Avis Milestone Achievement Award winners are publicized throughout the company. "Our Lead the Drive to Preeminence program has become a very important part of Avis's employee loyalty efforts," says Jim Keyes, vice president of human-resources staffing and diversity. "Our goal is to recognize more levels of performance than we ever have, to reach a more significant portion of the workforce. Employees can get a paycheck anywhere, but a company that offers appreciation will have a competitive advantage in the marketplace. We sincerely believe that.

The result of all this recognition?

Avis is enjoying high satisfaction levels on employee-attitude surveys, which it believes is directly contributing to outstanding financial success.

In short, how employees feel about their company and their jobs has a significant impact on the quality of their work, their relationship with management and their ability to adapt to change. Recognition and awards play a vital role in improving the relationship employees have with their organization and their leaders. Strategic recognition and awards programs can also play a key role in retaining top performers and enhancing performance with all your people.

To be strategic, to be effective, recognition must touch every employee in your company, it must be simple to administer, it must include compelling communication, it must have the support of every member of your senior management and it must be integrated under one cohesive umbrella.

PART THREE
CARROT HARVEST

"You can't always get what you want....
But if you try sometime, you might just find,
you get what you need."

— Mick Jagger, *Rock 'N' Roll Circus*

*What will offering the right carrots
do for your organization?*

*With the right recognition, your organization
will attract and develop more talent and
create greater value.*

Very rarely in our research have we found a company that has been successful long term that does not cultivate the loyalty of intelligent, hard-working people—individuals who drive innovation or efficiency.

Why don't more companies understand that?

Actually, most companies think they *are* cultivating employee loyalty.

Take, for example, our visit to the corporate offices of a major Fortune 100 company. Turnover statistics in numerous areas of the company were staggering. We didn't want to confront them about it directly, so we steered them into a conversation about their employees. Eventually, they said, "Yes, employees are grumbling. They are just upset because we can't pay them more."

They weren't even close.

If your company is like most in North America, you want higher profits and better cash flow, you want more business, you want satisfied customers who keep coming back, you want growth and opportunity, and you want employees who are committed, innovative and efficient.

But if you are like most organizations, you are missing the boat. To get all that in today's highly dynamic, complex and competitive environment, you must change the way you manage and reward people. You must give employees the essence of what they need.

No, it's not money or job security. Remember the Gallup Study? Those criteria weren't even in the top twelve. No, people want to work for a company that recognizes their unique contributions. According to one recent study, 88 percent of employees say their biggest beef with their organization is "not enough acknowledgement for their work."[22] Another survey showed that 70 percent of employees want improvements in recognition and awards before they will feel more committed to their organization.[23]

Recognition improves retention levels; it enhances personal worth; it builds relationships between management and employees. In short, if corporations treat their people better than the competition, they will attract and develop more talent and create greater value.

But even with the magnitude of proof and research that supports the human need for recognition, in crunch time managers ignore the carrots and instinctively go for the bread. Despite the fact that you'd have to dig pretty deep to find a more effective motivational tool than recognition, managers are often afraid to hand it out. Some are afraid it will make them seem "soft"; others are concerned that they will be seen as playing favorites; others are just too busy to say "thank you" or develop creative recognition and award programs; some don't know how.

But the truth is, the vast majority of managers still don't realize how important recognition is to employees. Managers assume that good wages and job security are of paramount importance. But employees say they want respect, inclusion and recognition of their contributions. Wages fall far, far down the list on most employee-satisfaction surveys.

In the first part of this book, we talked about the corporate need for carrots. In the second section, we looked at the elements of successful recognition. Now we'll address the underlying benefits of offering carrots to your people.

Let's Back Up: What Humans Need

To gain support, a leader must be able to understand and motivate people. But to understand and motivate people, he or she must understand human nature.

Abraham Maslow suggested that people do not act by mechanical or unconscious instinctual impulses.[24] Instead, he said, people strive to reach the highest levels of their capabilities. People seek the frontiers of creativity and attempt to reach the highest levels of consciousness and wisdom. Maslow also explained that basic human needs are arranged in a hierarchical order, and that in order to move up a level, our needs at the previous level must be somewhat satisfied.

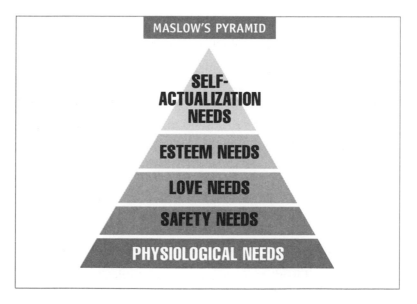

MASLOW'S PYRAMID

SELF-
ACTUALIZATION
NEEDS

ESTEEM NEEDS

LOVE NEEDS

SAFETY NEEDS

PHYSIOLOGICAL NEEDS

Individuals at the highest level of human behavior are healthy, creative people who use all their talents, potential and capabilities. Psychologists refer to these people as "fully functioning" or possessing a "healthy personality." Maslow called them "self-actualizing."

But most corporations leave their people's needs unfulfilled— and that leaves them feeling inferior, weak, helpless, even worthless.

Take the example of a young man we met while consulting with a large company. A graduate of a prestigious business school, the man was quite candid with us. He was regretting the choice of working for a big corporation; he had lost much of the confidence he possessed upon leaving business school and was considering moving to a smaller company where he'd really be "needed." We spoke to his manager. She said the young man had a bright future with the company if he could just get over his negative attitude.

Talk about a disconnect.

One of the key unfulfilled needs in the corporate world is the need for a stable, firmly based, high level of self-respect. And, as overwhelming as it may sound, your employees can't fully achieve that self-respect without your help. They need respect from others—and from you, in particular—in order to feel satisfied, self-confident and valuable.

Esteem needs are satisfied through status and recognition. But most traditional work environments do not typically lead employees toward esteem fulfillment. And because they do not feel needed and respected, many of today's employees develop feelings of anger and mistrust. Unfortunately for your company, that anger and mistrust grow like weeds through company walls, between floors, and across state lines. Soon the entire company can share the discontent.

Feeding the Rabbit Within Us

Frankly, a good part of corporate America distrusts its top management, is offended by their outlandish pay and stock options, openly questions their competence, and mocks their self-importance. And, quite simply, people don't stick around very long in organizations without trust. Leadership researchers James Kouzes and Barry Posner call trust "the most significant predictor of individual satisfaction with their organization."[25]

A lack of trust hurts organizations in a variety of subtle and not-so-subtle forms.

Here's what we found in a mid-sized western company. After circulating what seemed to be a fairly routine readership survey of internal publications, management began to discover a trust problem. The survey form contained a small number (different for each region) designed to allow data processing to monitor the response rate from various regions without identifying individual respondents. Throughout the organization, employees expressed outrage and disgust at management's "attempt to identify malcontents." The sharpest management members asked, "If employees didn't harbor strong feelings of mistrust toward us, would the reaction to an honest oversight have been so vitriolic?"

Shortly after that incident, in the same company, a similar reaction followed an announcement that employees at the head office would begin paying market rates for previously subsidized parking. Many employees grumbled about the "latest take-away" and management tipping the scales too far in favor of the shareholder at the expense of employees.

An unsigned letter was left on an executive's desk. It read: "When management continually professes its highest allegiance to shareholders, employee satisfaction becomes a whisper in the wind. The message becomes: 'Work harder, work longer, and be glad we treat you as good as we do. We really need employees, but we don't answer to them. Replace them, yes. Outsource their responsibilities, yes. Appease them, no.'"

By then, every member of the company's management team realized they had a significant problem with trust.

In the second part of this book, we paraphrased a line from Stephen Covey, a stream of logic that goes like this: The key to relationships is trust; the key to trust is credibility; the key to credibility is consistency.

To build trust, a company needs, first and foremost, consistent, sincere employee recognition. Companies need to manage with carrots. A few outstanding organizations throughout the world have figured that out and have built cultures that recognize individual and team accomplishments. These organizations report high levels of trust. They also have higher profits and lower turnover.

In fact, after decades of research on employee satisfaction, researchers Kouzes and Posner found that to get extraordinary things done in an organization, the best companies build a culture of trust and mutual respect by making use of a "human longing for meaning and fulfillment." In other words, the best organizations recognize the individual for his or her own important role in the organization's work. They inspire their workforce to act, and they reward the individual and the team.

That's what Warner-Lambert discovered when it began to support the basic human need to be appreciated. The company understood that long-term success would be built not with high-end strategy, by the wise use of capital, or even by pursuing such seemingly fundamental goals as customer satisfaction or shareholder return. Real success, they realized, would come only with buy-in and commitment from employees.

Now, we know what we're saying here can be threatening to some companies. It sounds so foreign. Changing corporate culture is always difficult. But in a way, the ideas we are espousing are ages old. Almost every senior executive (90 percent, according to a recent investigation) says that people are their company's greatest asset, and a full 98 percent declare that increasing productivity would enhance the bottom line.[26] But that's where it stops; it's just talk. Given the chance to rank the strategies most likely to bring success, executives put the people issues—performance and investment in the workforce—near the bottom.

One managing principal of Towers Perrin talked about a study of senior-executive attitudes. "They almost universally said people are the most important thing. But I asked them how their most important resource fit into the company's plans, and, without exception, they looked at me like I was from another planet," she said.

Dr. John Sullivan is a noted researcher on employee motivation. He says that recognizing the individual can result in measurable business results. In fact, he says, the companies that do employee recognition well often have turnover rates of 4 percent or less.[27]

"Realize it's not the money that drives people away," wrote Dr. Sullivan. "One firm tracked the difference in salary between what former employees were paid at their old jobs and what they earned at their new firms. They found the average salary differential was a little more than five percent. People don't leave their jobs for money."

Dr. Sullivan noted that companies with low turnover typically have good managers, and those managers provide employees with challenges, opportunities and confirmation that they make a difference, supported by recognition and awards.

Provide those, he said, and turnover will fall faster than a pair of cheap socks.

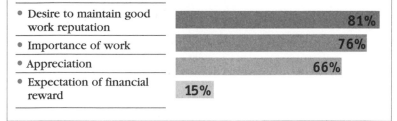

Source: *The New Employment Deals,* Strategic Rewards, *Watson and Wyatt survey of 551 large employers, April 2000.*

Carrots Vs. Cash

According to Naresh Agarwal, a professor of psychology at McMaster University in Hamilton, Ontario, reward systems can help influence two types of employee behavior: membership and performance.[28] "Membership" includes behaviors such as joining and remaining with the organization and coming to work regularly and punctually. "Performance" comprises the entire range of behaviors required in the performance of a job, especially as they align with corporate objectives.

The specific membership and performance behaviors necessary in a job depend on the organization. A "prospector" organization focuses on new products, markets and technologies and must reward creativity, risk-taking and team-based behaviors. A "defender" organization operates in stable markets and typically rewards efficiency, consistency and cost-saving behaviors.

Next, to be effective in influencing behavior, reward systems should satisfy three key requirements:

First, **awards should recognize only results that are important to the organization.** Too many organizations foul up this requirement. All of us have worked for or have known an organization that claims to value teamwork but rewards the person with the best individual performance; or an organization that wants its senior sales staff to mentor and train junior employees but rewards salespeople based solely on their personal perform-ance; or a university that wants professors to continually improve their teaching abilities but rewards and recognizes professors only for their research and publications.

Second, **awards should be fair.** That means, recognition awards should be fair in relation to awards received by equally producing coworkers and related to the significance of the achievement. Creating this type of fair reward is almost impossible with cash but much easier with tangible awards that have high perceived value.

Third, **awards should be of value to employees**. The logic of this is derived from Maslow's need theory and the Lawler/ Vroom expectancy theory. Both theories argue that individuals engage in behaviors that produce rewards that satisfy some salient need. Rewards have value to employees only when they satisfy a basic human need.

That's why most recognition programs use tangible awards that appeal to a basic instinct to want that which we do not have. We can picture ourselves wearing a beautiful piece of jewelry or an eye-catching ring. We can imagine just where that stunning Howard Miller mantel clock will go in our home. We think of how handy that Swiss Army knife would be on the next camping trip. We'd love to have that compact Sony camcorder for when the new baby arrives. We can visualize ourselves burning up the back nine with those new Callaway golf clubs.

And because we can picture the award and can imagine ourselves enjoying it, we are more likely to work harder to achieve it.

That's what Goodyear first discovered in 1994, when it sponsored a campaign to improve sales of tires in its North American operations.[29] Two large employee groups were monitored: One was offered monetary rewards, the other was offered merchandise. The group receiving tangible awards outperformed the cash-awards group by nearly 50 percent.

Why? Because cash is unemotional, and cash has been proven to have little power to motivate. Yes, many of your employees may tell you, "Show me the money." But according to the survey we cited earlier, 29 percent of your people will use cash gifts to pay bills. Another 18 percent will not even remember where they spent the money. Obviously, cash is not a solution for a company hoping to build a long-term bond with its employees.

Consider why you are rewarding your employees in the first place. Do you want them to connect their exceptional achievements and performance with your company's vision and goals? Do you hope the award will be a long-term reminder of accomplishments—of goals met and expectations exceeded? Should awards remind employees of their contributions to your company's success? Do you want the recognition to encourage other employees to excel? Should your awards and recognition be unmistakably tied to the value you place on quality employees?

If you answered "yes" to any of the above questions, you shouldn't even consider a cash-only award option.

Instead, consider the example of John Camiolo, director of global compensation for Warner-Lambert, who administered a global achievement program for his company's Pharma Sector. The achievement award was given every other year and rewarded individuals and teams for achieving key strategic goals for the sector. He used a combination of cash and awards.

Why both? Camiolo put it this way, "Like a lot of things in life, money comes and money goes, a memento is there to stay. It's not the award as much as the things around the award that you remember."

He added, "Cash is important, but people collect things, things that remind them of events and people and places. In the workplace, these things are a constant reminder of the team. They build esprit de corps, are constant reminders of the specific goal, and are easily recognized by others in the company."

Now, let's couple those benefits with the tax implications. In 1986, the U.S. Congress and President Reagan signed legislation that makes non-cash service and safety awards tax-free below an average companywide cost per employee of $400. Thus they are excludable

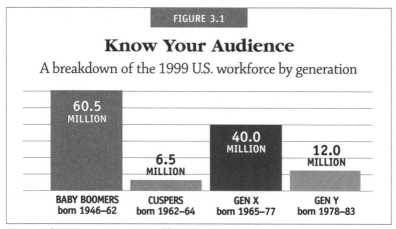

FIGURE 3.1

Know Your Audience

A breakdown of the 1999 U.S. workforce by generation

60.5 MILLION — BABY BOOMERS born 1946–62 · 6.5 MILLION — CUSPERS born 1962–64 · 40.0 MILLION — GEN X born 1965–77 · 12.0 MILLION — GEN Y born 1978–83

Source: "Who's in My Generation?" Workforce, November 1999. Source cited: Rainmaker Thinking, Inc., a New Haven, Connecticut–based consulting firm.

from the income of individual award recipients. Cash awards, on the other hand, are taxed as income, diminishing the value of the money.

"While money is probably the most universally desired reward, it is not the best recognition award because it has no symbolic value, and, once spent, there is nothing to remind the employee of the special event," says Dr. David J. Cherrington, a professor of management at Brigham Young University and the author of numerous books and research articles on organizational behavior and leadership. "The best awards are functional jewelry or office or home accessories that are made of precious metals (such as gold and diamonds) that contain some form of symbolism, such as the company logo or colors," he says.

In short, the best carrot is often a karat.

Carrot Cures for Generation X

They make up about 34 percent of the workforce, yet we understand so little about them. They are Generation X—born between 1965 and 1977—and recognizing this unique group takes a special approach.

For the most part, Generation-X workers are looking for daily proof that their work matters. That means recognition—frequent, meaningful recognition.

HR experts note that despite the media dubbing them slackers, Gen Xers are typically self-reliant and entrepreneurial in spirit. And while it's tough to keep this group motivated, it's not impossible.

First and foremost, Gen-X employees want to be involved in decision making. Forget the days of giving orders or leading the troops by example. To gain the heart and soul of your younger workers, you must learn to lead by interaction and inclusion.

That also means involving them when it comes time to reward their positive activities. According to Bruce Tulgan, president of the New Haven, Connecticut–based consulting firm Rainmaker Thinking, Gen-X employees want choices when it comes to recognition awards.[30] Managers, he says, should ask younger employees what awards they value. "Recipients will find rewards more compelling if they can be customized to fit their tastes."

SIDELIGHT

Measuring Carrots

If your company spends thousands or millions of dollars on a recognition program, your management team might want some evidence that the program is effective in meeting strategic company goals.

A survey can determine overall program satisfaction and verify program effectiveness. If necessary, it can also help justify a program's existence.

"A good survey measures all aspects of the recognition experience—from evaluating program communication to award satisfaction, from the effectiveness of the award presentation to overall program impact," says Greg Boswell, manager of market research for the O.C. Tanner Company and a member of the board of directors of the National Association for Employee Recognition.

Boswell, who has overseen the evaluation of hundreds of recognition programs, notes that, "While quantitative measurement is most critical to understanding a program's effectiveness, don't overlook asking an open-ended question or two to get additional feedback such as, 'What would have made your recognition experience more meaningful?' "

Many successful companies survey employees either after they have ordered their recognition awards or after awards are presented by their managers. Reactions help you gauge:

- Is the ordering process simple?

- Are we offering a popular selection of items?

- Are the program goals clear and effectively communicated?

- Was the award presentation memorable and positive?

- Has the program improved over the past few years?

- Are employees being recognized frequently enough?

- Does the program have areas for improvement?

Positive reactions can help you justify the current program. Negative responses can help you reshape your strategy or your execution.

In addition, company-wide, internal measurements will tell you which managers are not using the recognition program, if managers and peers are nominating others frequently enough, if program guidelines are being kept, and if recognition is becoming part of the culture of your organization.

However, the most important measurements of a recognition program show up in the bottom line as improvements in performance, sales, customer satisfaction and employee turnover. Here's a specific example. Kinko's says its recognition program and several other recent changes have helped the company realize a 33 percent reduction in employee turnover.

Your recognition program should also have a measurable impact on employee morale and feelings of appreciation—which could be measured with a baseline survey and then updates every 12 to 18 months.

Overall, your measurement program can help you understand whether employee attitudes about the company are improving and if recognition is actually driving organizational performance and strategic results.

Carrots for the Road: A Recognition Case Study

At Southern Wine and Spirits, the largest distributor of bottled waters, juices and alcoholic beverages in the United States, the first thought on drivers' minds is safety. It's also the second and third thing.

A safety-recognition award program has played a huge part in keeping that thought in the front of drivers' minds and has helped the company drop financial losses due to safety accidents by 70 percent—from almost a million dollars annually in the early nineties to a few hundred thousand dollars annually today.

Southern Wine & Spirits says the company's safety-award program has helped save 70 percent in claims related to injuries.

Mark Krauss is national director of HR for Southern. He says drivers are the company's biggest risk and safety challenge. Krauss developed a safety reward he knew would appeal to his drivers: a top-quality, Super Bowl–style gold-and-diamond ring.

To claim a gold ring, a Southern driver must remain absolutely safe—free from all accidents and safety-related problems—for five years. After that, one 10-point diamond is added to the ring for each year of continued safety. As a work in progress, the ring is a motivator not only for continued safety but also for continued employment at Southern.

Earning the ring took driver Alex Barnes nine years. At one time, with only six months to go, he got a traffic ticket and had to start the entire five-year process again.

"I didn't give up on it," Barnes says. "I wanted it so bad. I concentrated and in five years had no accidents and no tickets and I finally made it. It's a goal I set for myself. Not only for the ring, but to know that I am safe—that I am not hurt and I am not hurting anyone else. It's truly an honor to wear the ring."

PART FOUR
STARTING YOUR OWN CARROT CROP

Where to begin?

Determine your most basic human needs, set strategic goals,
choose the right awards, build excitement . . .
but keep it simple.

Up to now, we've given you just a taste of what carrots can do for your organization: greater, sustained productivity, high employee morale, amazing retention. Does just thinking about it make your mouth water? Then you're ready to plant your own carrot crop.

The great thing about carrots is their versatility. They're effective at any level, within any organization. It makes no difference whether you're the supervisor of two or three people, a senior manager, a human-resource leader or a top executive.

So, roll up your sleeves and let's get to work.

First Things First

First, understand that it is imperative to plant carrot seeds early: as early as the employee's first day at work.

Ray Fino, former senior vice president of global HR at a Fortune 50 company, tells the sad story of his own first day of work. Fresh out of college, he was excited to start his new career. He had made it through the interview process and was eager to impress his new employer. As the visions of "what could be" were flooding through his head, he was greeted on his first day at work by... no one. HR was not expecting him. His new department was not expecting him. No one knew what to do with him. As people fumbled to get him the right forms and find him a place to sit, he couldn't have been more disappointed. He says now that it was his first day at his new job and his first day of looking for his next job.

But imagine what happens to a newly hired employee when, in the first few days of her employ, she witnesses her colleagues receive or bestow recognition. Immediately, the new hire knows that this environment will be one in which people are recognized for accomplishments and also that such attention comes from multiple sources.

Would an environment like that have an effect on your ability to keep new employees? And answer this question: How would *your* first job have been different if that company had properly acknowledged your contributions and created a culture of recognition and encouragement from day one?

If you do it right, you have a much better chance of keeping those good employees. Otherwise, very different seeds can be sown on that first day: discontent, fear and instability.

Next, you've got to keep those carrots coming. There's a little bit of rabbit in all of us, constantly craving the sense that someone in authority acknowledges our best efforts. The best companies in North America feed their people recognition on a regular basis, satisfying a basic human need.

If you take nothing else away from this book, please understand this: By small but symbolic gestures of appreciation, you can improve the work lives of your employees. You create a sense that something greater than just the fulfillment of orders, products or services is going on at your place of work. You are creating a place where people are happy to spend their time, a place where people are proud to work.

Easy as One-Two-Three . . .

Whether your company occupies the smallest corner of its market or dominates the entire field, you need to cultivate a carrot culture. Here's the skinny on how to best implement a formal-recognition program:

Step One: **Dig Up Critical Company Data**

Perform a quick study of your organization. Identify your corporate culture, the makeup of your workforce and your most pressing human needs.

Step Two: **Plot Out Your Program**

Focus formal recognition on significant achievements and milestones. Begin early, recognize often and provide extra incentives for your best people. Develop communication that will link your corporate vision and mission to individual accomplishments.

Step Three: **Pick Your Carrots Wisely**

Select recognition awards that are appropriate for your employees, awards that provide personal, lasting value. Ensure that awards will provide the corporation with a return on its investment by developing a unique symbol or emblem that correlates individual achievement with company vision.

Step Four: **Create a Craving**

Gain full benefit from each award that is presented. Build excitement for the program with brochures, posters, videos and other promotional materials before the first award is presented. Provide training to your managers to help them make meaningful presentations.

Step Five: **Keep Carrots Within Reach**

Conserve the time of your managers and HR professionals. Develop a program with simple administration and award fulfillment.

Beware of missteps that detract from your goal of strategic recognition. Here are a few common errors:

Complexity. Some recognition programs are so complicated that no one bothers to participate. In one performance recognition program we evaluated, the nomination form was more detailed than an IRS tax document. To be part of a company's day-to-day culture, recognition programs must be simple for the nominating employee, the approving manager, the recipient, the presenting manager and the program administrator.

Lack of Timeliness. Some companies require committee approval before a recognition award is granted, others rigidly require all recognition to occur at a specific time— like a year-end banquet. But to be effective, recognition should be timely. That means approvals must be streamlined and presentations must be made within a few days or weeks of the accomplishment.

Lack of Buy-in. Recognition programs that don't get top-management buy-in are doomed from the start. Senior managers must be actively involved in the recognition process and must genuinely believe in the recognition program and its ultimate goals.

Lack of Integration: It's possible to get too much of a good thing—even carrots. Many companies find that out the hard way, after allowing numerous programs to be developed at random in various divisions and at a corporate level. After a time, they grow out of control—confusing employees and costing the company a great deal of misdirected money, while seldom moving employees toward the corporate vision or business objectives.

One company that invited us to consult had more than forty recognition programs. Most employees couldn't name a handful. After we had finished our work, the company had only two recognition programs: a wide-sweeping but integrated performance program and a meaningful service-award program. Today, all employees can name the current recognition programs, how and why someone is nominated, and what the recipient will receive. The process includes peer-to-peer and manager nominations as well as formal and informal recognition. The system is easy to understand and very public.

Lack of Preparation. Skillful award presentations can turn an ordinary, garden-variety carrot into solid gold. But too many companies leave this crucial element in the hands of their managers, providing little if any support. We've seen presentations where humor was used inappropriately, where the recipient's name was mispronounced, and where the wrong work accomplishments were spotlighted. For example, at one award presentation we witnessed, a manager went on and on about "Leslie's excellent work organizing the department picnic." While the presentation was certainly nice, we wondered if Leslie and her coworkers left the meeting with any better understanding of what type of activities the company valued.

Another common mistake is a presentation that is too casual. We stood on a cold loading dock one early morning as delivery drivers were about to be sent out for the day. The burly foreman ended the meeting by saying, "Oh, by the way, Doug's been here twenty-five years today. Way to go." The foreman then tossed a package at Doug. The foreman didn't mean any harm. But the worker caught the award, looked at it with disdain, and then tossed it back. Doug told us later, "If that's what twenty-five years mean to them, then they can keep the watch."

In contrast, we recently spoke at the retirement party of a good friend. Bob Gritman had been with the same company for more than thirty years. To say good-bye, his colleagues threw him a special dinner. Old colleagues were asked to attend, as was his family. It was a wonderful tribute to a valued and committed employee. The gifts that were presented were symbols of love and respect, treasures that he will enjoy for years to come. There was no check or cash; this was not the time or the place. Each award was thoughtful, and each presenter shared stories of his or her relationship with Bob and his family. Bob was very moved. So were his coworkers. They could see that he was valued and treated with respect, and from the faces of those in attendance, it was easy to see that they aspired to the same level of acknowledgement.

Never Underestimate a Carrot

No matter how you slice it, the truth is that carrots bring out the best in employees. That's why it's so important that personal, dignified recognition begins the moment employees enter your company. If you make them *feel* valuable, they are likely to prove to you that they *are* valuable. Continue showing respect, acknowledgement and recognition through consistent, fair and motivating presentations as long as your employees are with you. Upon retirement, cap off years of service with tributes that celebrate accomplishment, influence and legacy. If you do it, you will prosper, your employees will prosper, and your company will prosper.

O. C. Tanner Company's founder, Obert Tanner, was the first to identify this corporate need for recognition awards. "We were pioneers in this field," he wrote in his memoirs. While teaching philosophy at Stanford University in the 1930s and '40s, Tanner traveled throughout the United States—making the case that recognizing and motivating employees with quality awards would promote better employer/employee relations.

Of the company he built, now the premier recognition company in the world, Tanner noted, "I sometimes reflect that we put a drop of oil on the bearings of the free-enterprise system. We help companies run a little more smoothly, with a little less friction, cultivating a more friendly environment where people work."

Recognition for Obert Tanner revolved around the Golden Rule. He said, "Kindness is expressed in a company's desire to recognize and honor its people. Giving the productive years of one's life, most of the daylight hours of each working day, is a huge sacrifice. Awards inspire a high morale and better performance."

Our work with O. C. Tanner has taken us around this continent, into the halls of many of the world's largest companies. We have seen how recognition should be done and how it should not be done. We have seen examples that brought tears to our eyes and some that made us cringe. But perhaps the most poignant reminder of the power of recognition came as our company was fitting U.S. Olympic athletes for their team rings before the 2000 Sydney Games. At team processing in San Diego, we met the charismatic runner Marla Runyon—the only legally blind athlete to ever qualify for an Olympic Games.

We didn't seek out Marla; she found us. She wanted her team ring, before she tried on any of the clothing or other accessories being handed out to the athletes. She knew that ring would be the only lasting reminder of her remarkable accomplishment.

Marla said to us, "I told my coach, I've got to get the ring—we've got to go to the ring table first. When I put it on, it was the most beautiful thing. It symbolizes making the team, making it to the Olympics.

"The ring will be either on my finger or on a chain around my neck for the rest of my life. It's very special, something I will keep forever."

Marla summarizes it beautifully. Symbolic recognition awards are lasting. More than ever they increase a person's affiliation with an organization, generate pride, elevate work satisfaction, and establish trust between managers and employees.

The need for strategic recognition is timeless. It furthers your organization's goals and appeals to the most basic needs of its individuals.

Ah, the power of a carrot. There's simply no substitute. Sure, you can lure employees to your company with more bread and perks. But nothing holds and fulfills them like recognition.

Today, more than ever, managing by carrots is effective and inspired. Managing with carrots is divine.

Endnotes

[1]See Buckingham, M., and C. Coffman. *First, Break All the Rules.* New York: Simon & Schuster (1999).

[2]See "In & Out?" *Kudos* (April 1998). Source: Dartnell Corp. quoting Bureau of National Affairs and the *Wall Street Journal.*

[3]"Employee Tenure in 2000." U.S. Bureau of Labor Statistics (August 29, 2000).

[4]See "Strategic Rewards: New Deals for New Times." *Forbes* (July 3, 2000). Quoting Watson Wyatt Worldwide study.

[5]Society for Human Resource Management, 1997 Retention Practices Survey.

[6]See "Crossing the Bridge to Victory." *Kudos* (April 1998).

[7]Se "If You Think Salaries are High, Just Look at Turnover Costs." *Employee Benefit News* (April 15, 1998). Quoting William M. Mercer study.

[8]See Albertson, David. "Data Challenge Assumptions on Retention Issues." *Employee Benefit News* (October 2000). Quoting Development Dimensions Inter-national and U.S. Department of Labor.

[9]See "Top Firms Reveal Strategies for Keeping Top Talent." *HR Wir* (September 28, 1998). Quoting Conference Board survey.

[10]O. C. Tanner Employee Recognition Survey, 33,774 award recipients, 1998.

[11]See Morris, P. H., and D. L. Kanter. "Combating Cynicism in the Workplace." *National Productivity Review* (Autumn 1989).

[12]See "Employee Information Sharing." Department of Employment and Industrial Relations. Australian Government Publishing Service (1982).

[13]See Williams, H. A. "You Are Your Logo: Corporate Image Should Be a Reflection of the Reality." *Management Today* [UK (January 1998).

[14]See Spaeth, Tony. "New Faces; Corporate Identity." *Across the Board* (February 1997).

[15]O. C. Tanner Employee Recognition Survey, 16,964 award recipients, 1997.

[16]O. C. Tanner shipping statistics, 1999.

[17]See Bannon, Lisa. "The Hyped and the Hypeless: Fate of Two Films." The *Wall Street Journal* (July 5, 1995).

[18]See Flynn, Gillian. "Is Your Recognition Program Understood?" *Workforce* (July 1998).

[19]See Covey, Stephen R. *Principle-Centered Leadership*. New York: Simon & Schuster, 1991.

[20]See Luporter, Christine. "A New Purpose in Life: Communication as Retention Tool." *Journal of Employee Communication Management* (September/October 1999).

[21]See Kotter, John. "Leading Change: Why Transformation Efforts Fail." *Harvard Business Review* (March/April 1995).

[22]See "Guess What's Still #1?" *Kudos* 3:4. Quoting Adele B. Lynn, management consultant, Lynn Learning Labs, *HR Fact Finder* (December 1998).

[23]See "Time for a Change?" *Kudos* 3:2. Quoting *In Touch,* Minneapolis, *MN/HR Factfinder* (December 1998).

[24]Maslow, A. H. *The Hierarchy of Needs,* 1943.

[25]See Kouzes, J. M., and B. Z. Posner. *The Leadership Challenge*. San Francisco: Jossey-Bass, 1997.

[26]See Noble, B. P "At Work; The Bottom Line on People Issues." The *New York Times* (February 19, 1995). Quoting Towers Perrin study.

[27]See Sullivan, John. "What Labor Shortage? Hewlett-Packard, Cisco, Intel and Microsoft Think It's Easy to Attract and Retain the Best Employees. Do You?" *Human Capital Strategies and News* (September/October 1999).

[28]See Agarwal, Naresh. "Reward Systems: Emerging Trends and Issues." *Canadian Psychology* (May 1998).

[29]See Alonzo, Vincent. "The Trouble With Money." *Incentive* (February 1996).

[30]See Hays, Scott. "Generation X and the Art of the Reward." *Workforce* (November 1999).

In Search of ... Great Recognition Stories

If you know of a great recognition experience or
of a company that does recognition right, please
let us know.

Email your recognition success stories to
adrian.gostick@octanner.com or
chester.elton@octanner.com or send them
to Adrian Gostick, O. C. Tanner Company,
1930 S. State Street, Salt Lake City, UT 84115.
Please include your name, company, phone
number, mailing address and email address.

If we use your story in a future edition, we'll send you a **gold
carrot pin** and recognize you and your company in the book.

the authors

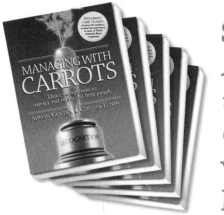

Share *Managing with Carrots* with Your Managers

To order copies of the book:

Telephone 1-800-748-5439
Or visit www.gibbs-smith.com

Discounts are available for orders of more than 25 books.